AMAZING FACTS, FUN PHOTOS, AND A LOOK-AND-FIND ADVENTURE!

BIGFOOT™

Goes on GREAT ADVENTURES

D. L. MILLER

Happy Fox
BOOKS™

For Mom and Dad, and the Miller brothers who grew up in our little house nestled in the mountains of Western Maryland, where we spent many a day exploring the beauty and mysteries of the woods and creek bottoms just outside our front door.

— D. L. Miller

A Big Thank You
to all the BigFoot hunters around the world who believe not only that our big furry friend really does exist, but more importantly that he continues to inspire us to go outside and explore this great big world.

A Special Thank You
to the wonderful folks at Fox Chapel Publishing for bringing the BigFoot Seek and Find series to life, especially…

Publisher: Alan Giagnocavo
Vice President–Content: Christopher Reggio
Senior Editor: Laura Taylor
Managing Editor: Melissa Younger
Contributing Editors: Anthony Regolino, Colleen Dorsey, Jeremy Hauck, Katie Ocasio
Graphic Designer: David Fisk

© 2019 by D. L. Miller and Happy Fox Books, an imprint of Fox Chapel Publishing Company, Inc., 903 Square Street, Mount Joy, PA 17552.

BigFoot Goes on Great Adventures is an original work, first published in 2019 by Fox Chapel Publishing Company, Inc.

ISBN 978-1-64124-025-3 (hardcover)
ISBN 978-1-64124-043-7 (paperback)

The Cataloging-in-Publication Data is on file with the Library of Congress.

To learn more about the other great books from Fox Chapel Publishing, or to find a retailer near you, call toll-free 800-457-9112 or visit us at *www.FoxChapelPublishing.com*.

We are always looking for talented authors. To submit an idea, please send a brief inquiry to acquisitions@foxchapelpublishing.com.

Fox Chapel Publishing makes every effort to use environmentally friendly paper for printing.

Printed in Malaysia

Shutterstock photos: 2C2C (19 top right); aarondfrench (39 middle right); acro_phuket (31 bottom center); ajt (43 middle-bottom right); Akugasahagy (42-43 open book); Albertus Bonke (22 bottom left); Alexandr Junek Imaging (35 middle right); Alex Polo (background: 40, 41); Alexey Suloev (10 top); Alfmaler (11 middle right); Alyona Naïve Angel (7 top left); Ammit Jack (7 bottom right); amskad (31 middle right); andamanec (35 bottom center); AndreAnita (39 bottom right); Anton_Ivanov (18 top right); April Cat (10 icicles); ArtMari (binoculars: 14, 30, 34, 42); Arto Hakola (15 bottom right); Audrey Snider-Bell (22 middle right); a_v_d (19 top left); Ben Queenborough (27 bottom left); BMJ (7 middle center); Brian Kinney (30 middle-bottom background); Chansom Pantip (22 top center leaves); chonlasub woravichan (31 middle left); CineBlade (4 top left); Circlephoto (27 middle center); Collin Quinn Lomax (7 top right); ComicSans (34-35 clouds); Cosmin Coita (background: 20, 21); Dan Bach Kristensen (39 top left); Dan Thornberg (7 middle right); Daniel Prudek (34 top background, bottom left; 35 bottom right; background: 36, 37); Delices (top left pin: 6, 10, 14, 18, 22, 26, 30, 34, 38, 42); Dennis van de Water (background: 16, 17; 14 bottom background; 15 top left); Dewin ' Indew (22 bottom right); divedog (31 bottom background); Don Mammoser (7 bottom left); Erofeeva Regina (35 middle right); EtiAmmos (11 middle center); evenfh (38 middle-bottom background); FentonPhotography (39 top background); Fitawoman (39 middle left); FJAH (26-27 bats); Fotoluminate LLC (6 bottom); Fotos593 (22 top-middle background); grass-lifeisgood (23 middle right); Greg291 (38 middle right); Horten (31 bottom left); ILYA AKINSHIN (bubbles: 30, 31); Jack Clancy (11 top right); Jasmine_K (26 top background); jorisvo (background: 44, 45); Joseph Sohm (38 middle left); Juli Hansen (top left topographic map: 6, 10, 14, 18, 22, 26, 30, 34, 38, 42); Katiekk (31 top left); Komjomo (background: 28, 29); kpboonjit (22-23 tree); Kurti afshen (15 bottom left); lendy16 (23 top right); Leonid Andronov (42 middle left-center); marekuliasz (6 top right); matrioshka (27 middle left); McLura (paint stroke: front cover, 1); Menno Schaefer (7 middle left); MichaelaS (15 middle left); MZPHOTO.CZ (11 top left); nega (42 middle center); nikolay100 (27 top far right); Nok Lek (15 top right); Nuamfolio (34 top right); Ognyan Biserov Nikolov (26 middle left); Olga Danylenko (35 middle-bottom left); Osugi (43 bottom left); pavalena (26 bottom left; 38 bottom left); Peter Hermes Furian (18 bottom); polarman (11 bottom left); Radu Bercan (14 bottom left); Rich Carey (30 middle center, 30 middle right); RikoBest (4 top right); Robert Spriggs (38 top background); Rudy Riva (4 bottom right); russ witherington (19 bottom background); rustamank (26 bottom right); R. Wellen Photography (42 top right); salajean (27 top left); saasemen (38 bottom right); schankz (background: 8, 9); Schwabenblitz (6 top center); Sean Pavone (43 top right); Sergey Lavrentev (5 top right); Sergio Schnitzler (43 top left); sevenke (43 yellow, blue, red open books); Slay (background: 12, 13); SL-Photography (23 top left); studiovin (42 bottom left); suthas ongsiri (18 top center, 19 middle center); Sylvie Bouchard (39 middle center); Tanya Puntti (30 middle left); Tarpan (10 bottom right); Tory Kallman (10 bottom left); Twin Design (43 bottom left); Twinsterphoto (background: 24, 25); Utir (5 map); Uwe Bergwitz (19 bottom left, bottom right); UWPhotog (background: 32, 33); VicW (39 snowflakes); Vilor (27 top center); Vixit (34 bottom right); vladsilver (11 middle left); Wang LiQiang (35 middle left); Weerachai Khamfu (27 middle center flames); xpixel (27 bottom right); zlatovlaska2008 (14 top right); Zzvet (35 top right)

BiGFOOT CONTENTS

Are you ready to explore the rainforest, raft down the Colorado River, and go mountain climbing?
BigFoot goes on great adventures, and you get to come along!

HOW TO USE THIS BOOK

Read about each amazing adventure.
You may learn something surprising!

Turn the page and search for BigFoot. The keys along the sides tell you what to look for. Good luck!

WHO IS BIGFOOT?

Stories about BigFoot have been around for years in many countries. Some people believe he's a **giant bear** that walks around on two legs. Other people think he may be a **giant gorilla**.

This picture is from the famous short video taken in 1967 in Northern California's **Six Rivers National Forest** by Roger Patterson and Bob Gimlin. Some people think this **BigFoot** was only a person in a costume. Others believe it's the real deal. What do you think?

BIG FOOT XING

DUE TO SIGHTINGS IN THE AREA OF A CREATURE RESEMBLING "BIG FOOT" THIS SIGN HAS BEEN POSTED FOR YOUR SAFETY

HAVE YOU SEEN A REAL BIGFOOT?

There are many stories about what BigFoot looks like. They all share some details: a big, furry, humanlike creature that is **7 feet (2.3 m) to 9 feet (3 m) tall**. Most people think BigFoot is brown, but many believe they have seen black, gray, white, or greenish-blue BigFoots. Some say he has **large eyes** and a **big forehead**. The top of his head might have the same shape as a gorilla. If you see someone walking around who looks like this, you're probably looking at BigFoot!

BigFoot might be able to run 30 miles per hour (48 kph). Most people run much, much slower!

WHERE DID THE NAME *BIGFOOT* COME FROM?

In the 1800s, the name *BigFoot* was first used for huge **grizzly bears** in the United States. **David Thompson** may have discovered the first real set of BigFoot footprints when he was hiking over the Rocky Mountains in 1811. The tracks were too big for even the largest bear. People later saw **huge footprints** in the forest that looked bigger than a large bear's. These footprints were about 24 inches (61 cm) long and 8 inches (20 cm) wide: twice as big as an adult shoe. Many people believe that these big footprints are proof that our BigFoot **really does exist!**

BiGFOOT GOES BY MANY NAMES

BigFoot has many names around the world, including the most common: Sasquatch. So don't forget to tell people you're going **"Squatching"** the next time you decide to search for our giant, furry friend. What do other parts of the world call BigFoot?

Barmanou
(Pakistan)

Basajuan (Spain)

Big Greyman
(Scotland)

Gin-Sung (China)

Hibagon (Japan)

Kapre (Philippines)

Kushtaka
(Alaska, USA)

Mapinguari
(Brazil and Bolivia)

Menk (Russia)

Moehau
(New Zealand)

Mogollon Monster
(Arizona, USA)

Orange Pendek
(Indonesia)

Skunk Ape
(Florida, USA)

Ucu (Argentina)

Waterbobbejaan
(South Africa)

Wendigo (Canada)

Woodwosa
(England)

Yeren (Mongolia)

Yeti (Russia)

Yowie (Australia)

COLORADO RIVER

ONE LONG RIVER

Starting in Colorado's Rocky Mountains, the Colorado River travels **1,450 miles** (2,334 km) to the Gulf of California. If you include the **tributaries** (streams) that branch out from it, this river touches **7 U.S. states** and 2 Mexican states.

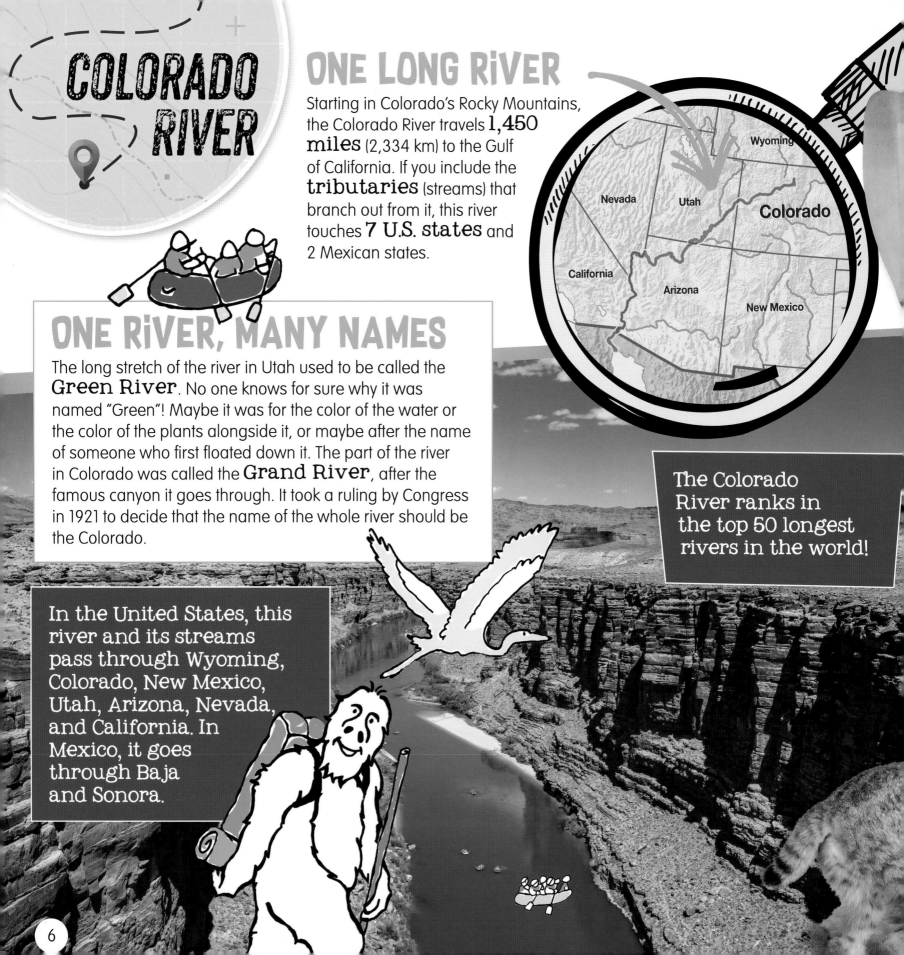

Wyoming

Nevada   Utah   Colorado

California

Arizona

New Mexico

ONE RIVER, MANY NAMES

The long stretch of the river in Utah used to be called the **Green River**. No one knows for sure why it was named "Green"! Maybe it was for the color of the water or the color of the plants alongside it, or maybe after the name of someone who first floated down it. The part of the river in Colorado was called the **Grand River**, after the famous canyon it goes through. It took a ruling by Congress in 1921 to decide that the name of the whole river should be the Colorado.

The Colorado River ranks in the top 50 longest rivers in the world!

In the United States, this river and its streams pass through Wyoming, Colorado, New Mexico, Utah, Arizona, Nevada, and California. In Mexico, it goes through Baja and Sonora.

RAPID RIVER ADVENTURES

Looking at this river is amazing, but floating on it is spectacular! Use a **kayak**, **paddleboard**, or **raft** for a river adventure. There are calm spots where it's easy to paddle around. And there are rough **whitewater** areas. That's where only the experts can raft the rapids without tipping over and falling in!

Rapids are the parts of a river where the water moves very quickly, usually over rocks.

A curve in the river created this cool spot that tourists love to visit. It has the perfect name: Horseshoe Bend!

Life jackets are a MUST when rafting—even for your daring doggie!

RAFTING HISTORY

In the **1840s**, John Fremont and Horace H. Day built the first rubber raft to explore the rivers of the American West. Whitewater rafting for fun became popular after rafters raced in the **1972 Olympic games** in Munich, Germany.

ANIMALS AT THE RIVER

Red-tailed hawks are expert hunters that can see a mouse from 100 feet (30 m) up in the air. These hawks are fast, too! They can streak across the sky at 120 miles per hour (193 kph). **Bobcats** are nocturnal (active at night), so you probably won't see one when you're rafting down the river. They are about twice as big as your pet cat. You may also see a fox. Baby foxes are called **kits**.

BiGFOOT
FOUND RAFTING THE COLORADO RIVER

1 BigFoot

1 Legendary Footprint

7 Graceful Great Blue Herons

5 Kayakers with Orange Kayaks

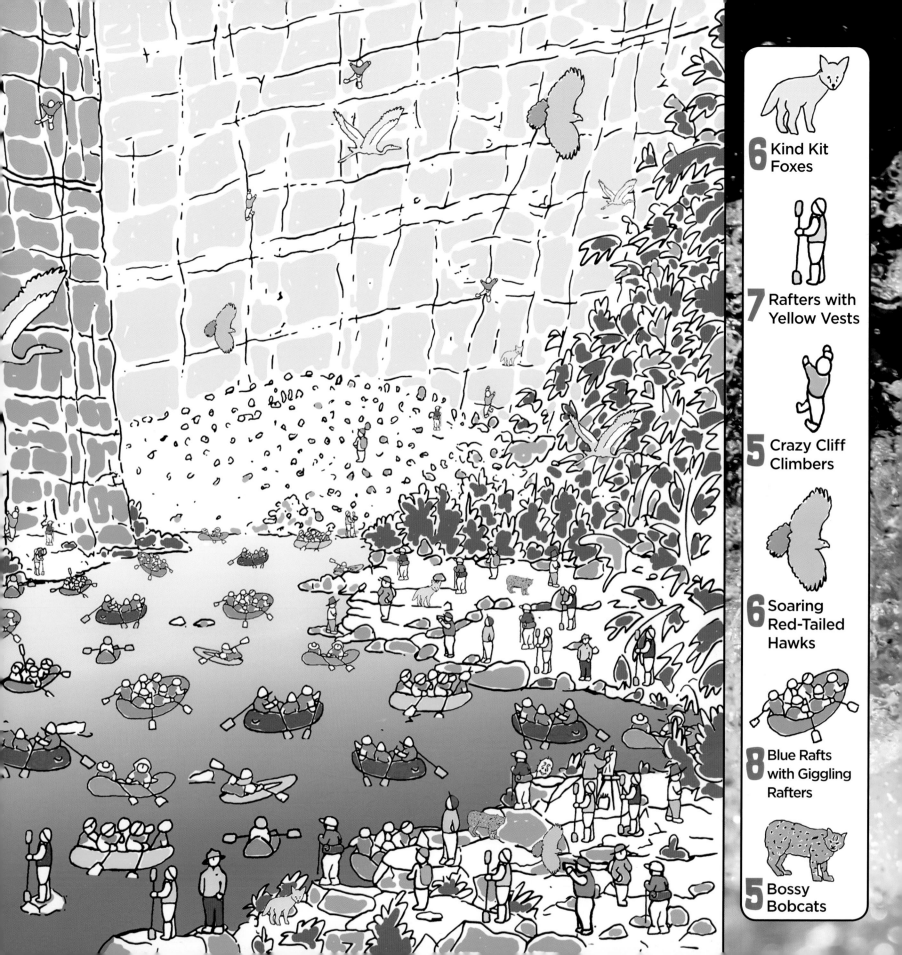

6 Kind Kit Foxes

7 Rafters with Yellow Vests

5 Crazy Cliff Climbers

6 Soaring Red-Tailed Hawks

8 Blue Rafts with Giggling Rafters

5 Bossy Bobcats

ANTARCTICA

EXTREME CONTINENT

Antarctica is at the most southern part of the Earth—it's where the **South Pole** is! Even with all of that snow and ice, it is a desert because there's so little precipitation (rain, sleet, snow, or hail that falls from the sky). Antarctica has an active volcano called **Mount Erebus**. It has a red-hot "**lava lake**." You don't want to stand near this dangerous lake—it sometimes spits out a lava bomb!

A continent is a very large piece of land. The Earth has 7 continents: North America, South America, Europe, Africa, Asia, Australia, and Antarctica.

COOL ANIMALS

Antarctica is the coldest place on Earth. The average winter temperature is -30°F (-34.4°C).

Over 1 million **emperor penguins** live on the shores of Antarctica. They are the largest kind of penguin: up to 45 inches (114 cm) tall and 88 pounds (40 kg). Male emperor penguins (not the moms!) will keep an egg warm until it hatches. **Orca whales** hunt together in groups called "pods." They can live up to 90 years in the wild. Males can weigh up to 19,000 pounds (9,000 kg) and females up to 12,000 pounds (5,500 kg). **Weddell seals** are very calm animals and spend much of their time in the water below the ice. Because they need air to breathe, they use their teeth to chip holes in the ice to breathe through.

Weddell seal

THEY COME AND THEY GO

While tourists and scientists visit Antarctica, there are no people who live there all the time. Antarctica doesn't have its own government. No country in the world can claim to own this land. Since 1959, many countries have agreed to keep Antarctica a safe, **peaceful place** to visit.

Albatross

Roald Amundsen, an explorer from Norway, was the first person to reach the South Pole. He arrived there on December 14, 1911.

ONLY TWO SEASONS

Due to the way the **Earth tilts** in space, Antarctica gets a ton of sunshine or none at all! In the summer, there are a few weeks when the **sun never sets**. And in the winter, there are weeks when it looks like nighttime all day long. Starting in May, winter lasts about **6 months** in Antarctica. Summer starts in November and lasts about 6 months.

If you're interested in meteorites, Antarctica is for you. Since 1976, there have been more than 20,000 meteorites discovered there.

There are no trees or bushes in Antarctica!

BiGFOOT
SPOTTED
IN ANTARCTICA

1 BigFoot

1 Legendary Footprint

17 Majestic King Penguins

9 Silly Southern Giant Petrels

13 Soaring Snow Petrels

8 Adorable Baby Seals

15 Totally Awesome Adélie Penguins

6 Very Sleepy Weddell Seals

20 Fluffy Baby Emperor Penguins

6 Curious Orca Whales

MADAGASCAR

ROCKY NATURE RESERVE

Madagascar is an **African island** in the Indian Ocean. It has lots of unique animals and land forms. One of the coolest landscapes is the **Tsingy de Bemaraha Integral Nature Reserve**. It has a maze of tall and pointy limestone rocks called *tsingys*. There are many canyons, caves, and tunnels that make it tough to travel through the area.

A **reserve** is land where nature is given special protection.

A **mammal** has a bony spine and skeleton, is warm blooded, usually has skin covered with hair, and feeds its young with its own milk. Human beings and many animals are mammals.

See if you can find BigFoot when he visited the African Plains! Check out *BigFoot Goes on Vacation.*

FANTASTIC FOSSAS

The **fossa** is a mammal that lives only in the rainforests of Madagascar. They are related to the **mongoose** but look more like cats. They have retractable claws and catlike teeth. They are the largest **carnivores** (meat eaters) in Madagascar.

MALAGASY PEOPLE

The people of Madagascar are known as **Malagasy**. When they wear traditional clothes, both men and women wear the same thing: a long, rectangular cloth that is wrapped around the body. This piece of clothing is called a *lamba*.

Madagascar is the fourth-largest island in the world.

TERRIFIC TENRECS

Tenrecs that live near the water have **webbed feet**, perfect for swimming. When another animal tries to catch them, tenrecs roll up into a **spiky ball**. Those **quills** are a sharp suit of armor!

LEAPING LEMURS

Madagascar is the only place in the world where you'll find lemurs in nature! Some lemurs have blue eyes: they are the only **nonhuman primates** that have them! Did you know that a lemur has **two tongues**? One to help them eat and a smaller one to groom (clean) other lemurs.

Primates are mammals with hands and feet that can grasp, a large brain, and vision that sees in 3D.

Madagascar has 59 species (kinds) of chameleons that don't exist anywhere else on Earth.

MACHU PICCHU

MOUNTAIN CITY

Machu Picchu is a very old **Inca city** in the Andes Mountains in Peru, a country in South America. In the 1400s, the Inca ruled from **Ecuador** to **Chile**. The empire covered 2,500 miles (4,000 km), which is almost how wide the United States is! The Inca used the city of Machu Picchu for religious ceremonies, as a military fort, and as a place for royalty to live.

Machu Picchu means "Old Mountain" in Quechua.

Peru declared independence from Spain in 1821. The country's bicentennial (200-year birthday) is in 2021.

VENEZUELA

COLOMBIA

GUYANA

SURINAME

French Guiana (FRANCE)

ECUADOR

PERU

BRAZIL

BOLIVIA

PARAGUAY

CHILE

URUGUAY

ARGENTINA

QUECHUA LANGUAGE

Spanish is the official language of Peru. But 10 percent of the people there speak **Quechua** (pronounced "ke-chu-wa"). Quechua was the language of the Inca Empire.

LLAMA VS. ALPACA

Both live in South America and are related to the camel, but there are differences! A llama's face is longer, and an alpaca's ears are shorter. Llamas can weigh up to 400 pounds (181 kg). Alpacas weigh around 150 pounds (68 kg). Alpacas tend to be a little shy, but llamas can be used to guard small animals. And alpaca wool is softer than a llama's wool.

Llama

Alpaca

Peru has a population of 31 million people. A person from Peru is called a Peruvian.

SOLID WALLS

The **buildings** of Machu Picchu were made of **stones** that were cut and put together **very tightly**. Not even a credit card could fit between them when they were built! There's **no cement** between the stones. So when an earthquake hits, the stones can wiggle instead of falling down.

STRONG BUT SHORT EMPIRE

The Inca Empire began in the early 1400s and quickly grew beyond Peru. Then, in the early 1500s, Spanish explorers and soldiers arrived, bringing disease and war. The Inca Empire ended in 1572, when the last ruler, Tupac Amaru, was killed by Spanish soldiers.

Statue of Inca ruler Pachacutec, who led the building of Machu Picchu.

BIGFOOT
VISITS AMAZING MACHU PICCHU

1 BigFoot

1 Legendary Footprint

5 Brilliant People from Peru

4 Slow-Moving Spectacled Bears

9 Super-Fast Giant Hummingbirds

9 Very Detailed Inca Pottery Bowls

8 High-Soaring Andean Condors

12 Amazing Alpacas

11 Loopy Llamas

4 Smiling Sun Symbols

AMAZON RAINFOREST

HOW RAINY IS A RAINFOREST?

Rainforests do get lots of rain: over **80 inches** (203 cm) a year and often much more. The Amazon rainforest in South America is the **largest tropical rainforest in the world**. It is humid and warm all year round.

FILLED WITH ANIMALS

A rainforest is an **ecosystem**, or a group of plants and animals living together. This ecosystem has 3 levels: **canopy** (top), **understory** (middle), and **forest floor** (bottom).

Canopy Critters:
macaws, toucans, howler monkeys, orangutans, sloths

Understory Cuties:
butterflies, snakes, plus palms, flowers, banana trees

Forest-Floor Furries:
jaguars, capybaras, tapirs (and maybe BigFoot?)

The Goliath birdeater tarantula can grow to 12 inches (30 cm) across. It rubs its hairy legs together to make a hissing noise. It's saying, "Back off!"

The jaguar is the biggest cat in South America. Unlike most cats, it's a great swimmer.

The Amazon rainforest stretches across 9 countries: Brazil, Bolivia, Peru, Ecuador, Colombia, Venezuela, Guyana, Suriname, and French Guiana. The biggest chunk—about 60%—is in Brazil.

Toucans' bills are mostly hollow and made of keratin. That's the same protein material in your fingernails.

AMAZING AMAZON RIVER

This rainforest surrounds the Amazon River, which runs from the **Andes Mountains** in the west to the Atlantic Ocean in the east. The Amazon River is the **biggest river in the world** because of how much water flows from it into the ocean.

PRECIOUS TREES

The Amazon rainforest is affected by **deforestation**. This is when trees are cut down and the land is used for farming or for building towns. Since the late 1970s, the Amazon rainforest has shrunk by **289,000 square miles** (750,000 km²). Forests help keep **carbon** in the ground so our planet stays cool. Without trees, lots of carbon gets into the air, making the Earth hotter and harder to live on.

The howler monkey's howl can be heard up to 3 miles (5 km) away.

The Amazon rainforest covers over 2 million square miles (5 million km²). It's almost the size of Australia!

BiGFOOT
VISITS THE AMAZON RAINFOREST

1 BigFoot

1 Legendary Footprint

6 Happy Howler Monkeys

11 Amazing Flying Toucans

10 Goliath Birdeater Spiders

5 Curious Capybaras

13 Brilliant Blue Morpho Butterflies

4 Super-Sneaky Jaguars

7 Majestic Flying Macaw Parrots

6 Terrific Tapirs

BULGARIA

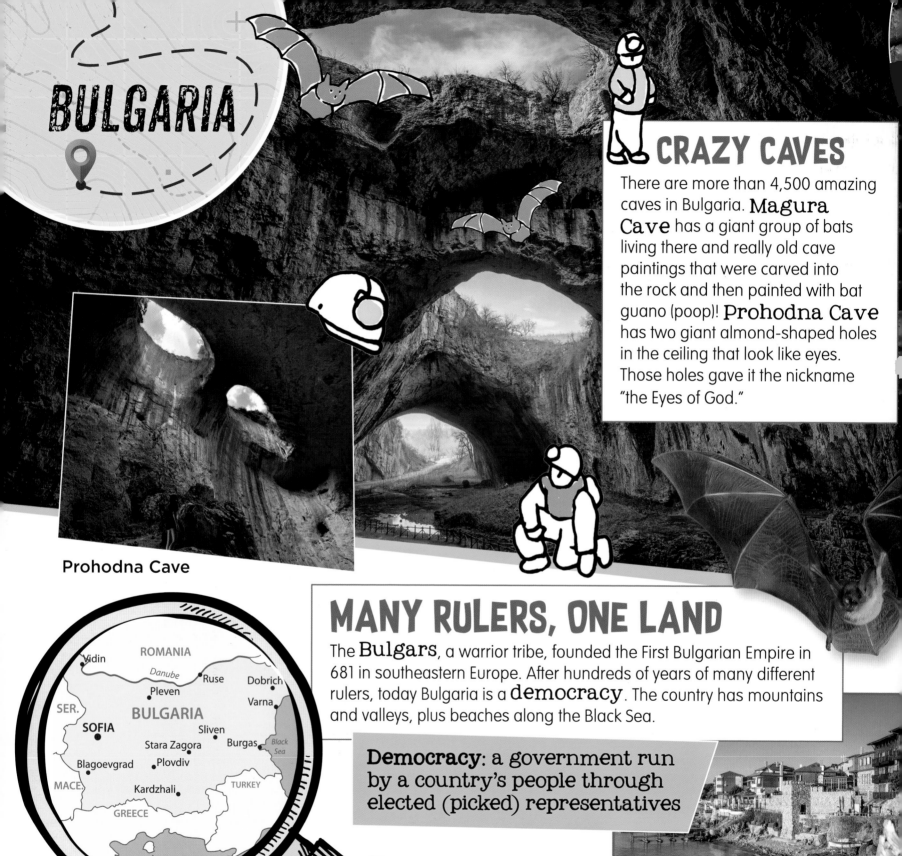

CRAZY CAVES

There are more than 4,500 amazing caves in Bulgaria. **Magura Cave** has a giant group of bats living there and really old cave paintings that were carved into the rock and then painted with bat guano (poop)! **Prohodna Cave** has two giant almond-shaped holes in the ceiling that look like eyes. Those holes gave it the nickname "the Eyes of God."

Prohodna Cave

MANY RULERS, ONE LAND

The **Bulgars**, a warrior tribe, founded the First Bulgarian Empire in 681 in southeastern Europe. After hundreds of years of many different rulers, today Bulgaria is a **democracy**. The country has mountains and valleys, plus beaches along the Black Sea.

Democracy: a government run by a country's people through elected (picked) representatives

ROMANIA
Vidin
Danube • Ruse
Pleven • Dobrich
SER. Varna
BULGARIA
SOFIA Sliven
Stara Zagora • Burgas Black Sea
Blagoevgrad • Plovdiv
MACE. Kardzhali TURKEY
GREECE
Aegean S

Bulgaria is about the size of the state of Tennessee.

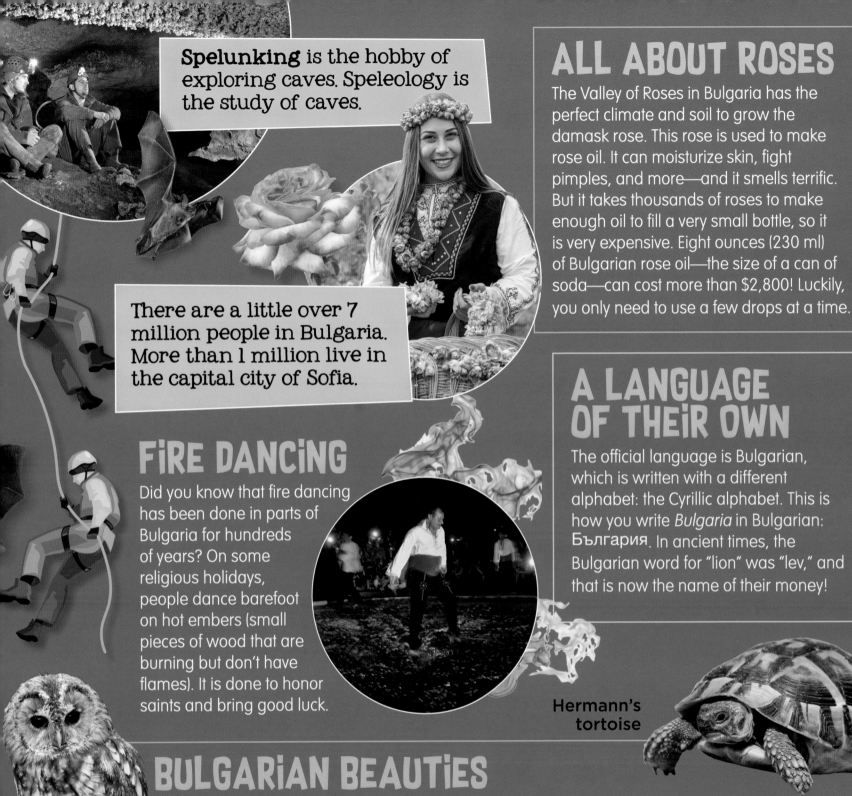

Spelunking is the hobby of exploring caves. Speleology is the study of caves.

There are a little over 7 million people in Bulgaria. More than 1 million live in the capital city of Sofia.

ALL ABOUT ROSES

The Valley of Roses in Bulgaria has the perfect climate and soil to grow the damask rose. This rose is used to make rose oil. It can moisturize skin, fight pimples, and more—and it smells terrific. But it takes thousands of roses to make enough oil to fill a very small bottle, so it is very expensive. Eight ounces (230 ml) of Bulgarian rose oil—the size of a can of soda—can cost more than $2,800! Luckily, you only need to use a few drops at a time.

A LANGUAGE OF THEIR OWN

The official language is Bulgarian, which is written with a different alphabet: the Cyrillic alphabet. This is how you write *Bulgaria* in Bulgarian: България. In ancient times, the Bulgarian word for "lion" was "lev," and that is now the name of their money!

FIRE DANCING

Did you know that fire dancing has been done in parts of Bulgaria for hundreds of years? On some religious holidays, people dance barefoot on hot embers (small pieces of wood that are burning but don't have flames). It is done to honor saints and bring good luck.

Hermann's tortoise

BULGARIAN BEAUTIES

When you walk through Bulgaria's forests and grasslands, you'll see **Hermann's tortoises**. They sleep in burrows at night and lie in the sun during the day. The **tawny owl**, found in Bulgaria and all over Europe, gets its name from its brown plumage (feathers). This owl's excellent hearing tells it exactly where its prey is.

Tawny owl

5 Happy Hermann's Tortoises

8 Super-Duper Spelunker Helmets

5 Totally Awesome Tawny Owls

8 Easygoing European Tree Frogs

3 Pondering Spelunkers

10 Fast-Flying Bats

THE GREAT BARRIER REEF

WORLD'S LARGEST CORAL REEF SYSTEM

The Great Barrier Reef is in the **Coral Sea** near Queensland, Australia. The Great Barrier Reef Marine Park stretches over **133,000 square miles** (344,400 km²). That's about half the size of Texas! Astronauts can see this reef from space. Around **1,500 kinds of fish live here**, including the tiny stout infant fish (¼ inch/7 mm long) and the huge whale shark (up to 34 feet/12 m long).

The Maori wrasse fish is one of the largest in the Great Barrier Reef and can live up to 30 years.

Maori wrasse fish

Coral trout

Butterfly fish

Bigfoot loves being in water. He had a great time deep sea diving (*BigFoot Goes on Vacation*).

TERREEFIC REEFS!

A coral reef may look like a bunch of rocks, but it's not! It's made of tiny animals called **polyps** that eat **plankton** and **algae**. When the polyps die, they get hard and new polyps grow on top of them—this makes the reef grow in size. **Reefs grow very slowly**—about ½ inch (1.3 cm) per year.

AUSTRALIAN HUMPBACK DOLPHIN

An Australian humpback dolphin has a small hump under its small dorsal fin (*dorsal* means "on the back" of something). Did you know dolphins use echolocation to find food? They make a high-pitched sound that bounces off an object and comes back. Using these echoes, dolphins can sense the location, size, and shape of an object.

A **turtle** spends most of its time in or near water. A **tortoise** lives on land.

Surgeonfish, or tangs, are named for their two sharp spines (like a surgeon's scalpels) by their tail.

LEATHERBACK SEA TURTLE

The leatherback sea turtle is the **largest sea turtle**, and weighs around **2,000 pounds** (900 kg). That's about the same weight as a **hippopotamus**! Leatherback sea turtles spend most of their time in the ocean. The only time a female will come to the shore is when she lays her eggs.

Over 2 million people visit the Great Barrier Reef each year. Would you like to dive in and see it up close?

White coral is dying coral.

Pollution and climate change are hurting the Great Barrier Reef. Help take care of your world: recycle, don't waste water, and turn off lights when you leave a room!

1 BigFoot

1 Legendary Footprint

10 Crazy Cardinal Fish

6 Totally Awesome Coral Trout

8 Massive Maori Wrasse Fish

10 Beautiful Butterfly Fish

6 Curious Snorkeling Dudes

5 Happy Humpbacked Dolphins

4 Peaceful Leatherback Turtles

14 Silly Surgeonfish

HIMALAYAN MOUNTAINS

BigFoot saw a mountain with famous faces carved into it: Mount Rushmore (*BigFoot Spotted at World-Famous Landmarks*).

MARVELOUS MOUNTAINS

The Himalayas are a mountain range **1,500 miles** (2,400 km) long. It crosses five countries: **Nepal, India, Bhutan, China,** and **Pakistan.** These mountains have the third-largest amount of ice and snow in the world, after Antarctica and the Arctic. There are about 15,000 glaciers (huge, solid pieces of ice) here. But it's not all chilly. The bottom of many of these mountains is warm and rainy in the summer.

WEATHER WALL

Because they're so **tall,** the Himalayas really affect the climate. They block the cold air from the north, so **India stays warm.** They also block the wet, warm air from the south, so **Tibet stays cool** and dry.

Climate is the pattern of weather in an area over many years.

THE BIG ONE: MT. EVEREST

Mt. (or "**Mount**") Everest is the highest mountain in the world. It is **29,029 feet** (8,848 m) tall and is in the Himalayas in Nepal. The top section of Mt. Everest is covered in snow that never melts. People first began trying to climb to the top of the mountain in 1921. **Not until 1953 did two people reach the top:** Edmund Hillary and Tenzing Norgay.

The Himalayas cover about 75% of the country of Nepal.

The Tiger's Nest Monastery is a Buddhist temple in the Himalayas of Bhutan. On the hike there, you'll see hundreds of colorful Buddhist prayer flags. They are hung as a way to hope for protection, energy, and other blessings.

EXPERT CLIMBERS

The **Sherpas** are a group of about 150,000 people who mostly live to the **south of Mt. Everest**. Before the 1900s, Sherpas did not climb the peaks of the Himalayas. They believed the mountains were the home of the gods. Today, many Sherpas act as guides to help others respectfully and carefully climb these beautiful but dangerous mountains.

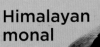
Himalayan monal

Lions, tigers, jaguars, and leopards are called "big cats." Snow leopards are the only big cats that can't roar.

Himalayan black bear

Himalayan tahr

Snow leopard

"HIMALAYAN" CREATURES

There are many animals that live mostly in the Himalayas, so they are named after the mountains! The **Himalayan monal** is the national bird of Nepal. The **Himalayan tahr** is a wild goat that lives on the slopes of the mountains. Their hooves have a rubbery center that helps them grip rocks. The **Himalayan black bears**, or moon bears, have a crescent moon-shaped patch of white on their chests.

Most big airplanes fly at 35,000 feet (12,000 m)—only a little higher than the top of Mt. Everest!

1 BigFoot

1 Legendary Footprint

5 Happy Hikers

8 Brilliant Himalayan Monals

10 Perched Buzzards

7 Hill-Climbing Himalayan Black Bears

5 Very Proud Snow Leopards

5 Resting Red Pandas

7 Adventurous Himalayan Tahrs

ALASKAN WILDERNESS

THE LAST FRONTIER

Alaska ranks at the top of many lists! It is the **coldest state in America**. The winter temperature can get down to -50°F (-46°C). Alaska is the **largest state** by land area: 665,384 square miles (1,723,000 km²). The highest peak in North America is here, too: Denali. It is 20,320 feet (6,194 m) above sea level.

Alaska compared to the size of 48 states

Alaska

Lower 48

Alaska became a state on January 3, 1959.

WILD WILDERNESS

About **half** of America's wilderness is in Alaska. A wilderness is a place where nature hasn't been changed by people. Alaska's wilderness has **spruce**, **birch**, **aspen**, and **cottonwood** trees. Many kinds of animals live here: moose, bear, red fox, caribou, hare, and more.

ARCTIC OCEAN

Beaufor

St. Lawrence

ALASKA

CANADA

Fairbanks

Kenai

Anchorage

Homer

Gulf of Alask

Kodiak Island

To be called a "wilderness," the area can't have roads, hotels, or stores. Snowmobiles and dogsleds are allowed.

You can also see these lights in Antarctica near the South Pole. They're called the Southern Lights.

An Arctic hare can run up to 40 miles per hour (64 kph). That's one hasty hare!

LOVELY LIGHT SHOW

The **Northern Lights** are an amazing, natural light show you can see at night when you're in Alaska. The best time to see them is from **September to April**. They look like a curtain of green lights, but they can sometimes be purple, red, or blue.

Musk ox

A baby caribou can walk about 1 hour after it's born!

Arctic tern

ALASKAN ANIMALS

A **grizzly bear** looks different from other bears because of its large shoulder hump, very long front claws, and the shape of its large head. **Grizzlies** are **omnivores**: they eat both meat and plants. They can weigh 770 pounds (350 kg) or more. **Musk oxen** are herbivores (plant eaters) that have two coats of hair to keep them warm. When hunted by wolves, musk oxen will make a circle with their young in the center and the adults' sharp horns facing outward. The **Arctic tern** spends most of the year at sea, where it eats small fish, crustaceans (like shrimps, crabs, and lobsters), and insects.

Grizzly bear

1 BigFoot

1 Legendary Footprint

7 Mighty Musk Oxen

5 Crazy Jumping Arctic Foxes

10 Rowdy Caribou

8 Serious Snowy Owls

8 Awesome Arctic Terns

4 Peaceful Grizzly Bears

14 Slowly Falling Snowflakes

6 Adorable Hares

LIBRARY OF CONGRESS

FOR THE PEOPLE

The Library of Congress was **created in 1800** and was in the Capitol building in **Washington, D.C.** It was only used by lawmakers. During the War of 1812, British soldiers set fire to the Capitol, and the Library's 3,000 books were destroyed. On January 30, 1815, Congress decided to build a new library by buying Thomas Jefferson's collection of **6,487 books for $23,950** (nearly $400,000 in today's money). By the late 1800s, the Library of Congress wasn't just for Congress. The American people could also use the Library.

Statue of Thomas Jefferson

The Library of Congress is the largest library in the world! It has 167 million items on about 838 miles (1,349 km) of shelves.

The **Capitol** is the building where the U.S. Congress meets. A **capital** is the location of a government. So the Capitol is in Washington, D.C., which is the capital of the United States.

The Capitol

BigFoot was a busy tourist in Washington, D.C., in *BigFoot Goes on Big City Adventures.*

A SPECTACULAR SEEK AND FIND CHALLENGE FOR ALL AGES!

BiGFOOT Goes on BIG CITY Adventures

D. L. MILLER

MEGA LIBRARY

Everything doesn't fit into just 1 building! The Library is in **3 buildings** in Washington, D.C.: the **Thomas Jefferson Building** (opened in 1897), the **John Adams Building** (built in 1938), and the **James Madison Memorial Building** (built in 1981). The Library also keeps items at the High Density Storage Facility in Fort Meade, Maryland, and in the Packard Campus for Audio Visual Conservation in Culpeper, Virginia.

WHAT'S INSIDE?

This amazing Library is home to all kinds of things! It has millions of **books, maps, photos, sheet music**, and recordings like **movies** and **music**. You can find some of these same things at your own school or town library. But some items are rare and can only be found at the Library of Congress. One example is the first book printed in North America: *The Bay Psalm Book* from 1640.

The oldest written item in the Library is a stone tablet from 2040 BCE.

MAIN READING ROOM

Anyone who is at least **16 years old** may use the Library's Main Reading Room in the Thomas Jefferson Building. It has thousands of reference books with facts about nearly anything you can think of. The room is also where expert librarians help people find the information they're looking for. Which book do you think **BigFoot** would like to read?

One of the Library's treasures is a perfect edition of the Gutenberg Bible, printed in the 1400s.

CHECK IT OUT

While you're welcome to visit the Library, you're not allowed to take any books home. It is a **research library**, so books can only be used in the building for studying. People of any age can tour the beautiful Thomas Jefferson Building, though. It has **marble floors**, a **stained glass ceiling, mosaics**, and **paintings**.

Visit your local library! You can find books about exciting places all around the world.

ANSWER KEY

Even on great adventures across the world, far from his home habitat, BigFoot is an expert at staying lost. He climbs roofs, hides behind buildings, blends into crowds—it's tricky work finding him! If you were stumped the first time around, you can use this guide—the **small red dot** shows where his elusive footprint is, while the **big red dot** in each picture reveals BigFoot himself. Just as in real life, the people, animals, and objects are easier to spot than finding BigFoot, so they are not included in this answer key.

BigFoot

Legendary Footprint

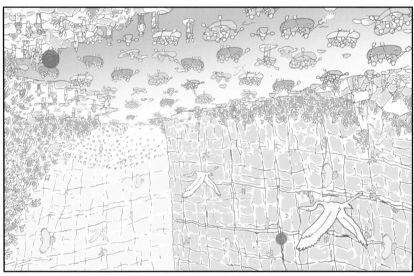

Colorado River

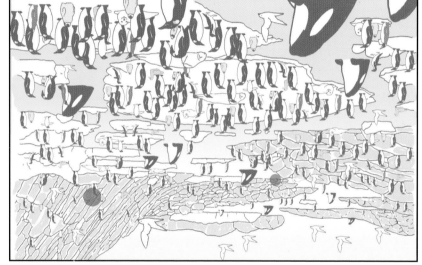

Antarctica

Madagascar

Machu Picchu

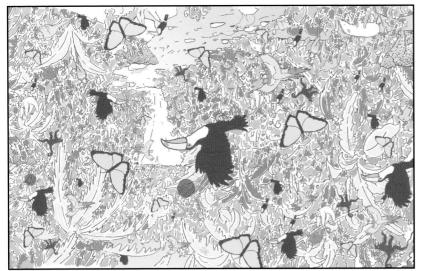

Amazon Rainforest

Bulgaria

Great Barrier Reef

Himalayan Mountains

Alaskan Wilderness

Library of Congress

ABOUT THE ARTIST

As with BigFoot, the artist and creator of this series is a bit on the elusive side. He is rarely seen in public, spending most of his days sketching in his studio, located among the mighty oak trees found only in the deep, dark woods far off the beaten path.

Deeply inspired by nature, the artist spent most of his childhood tracking creatures great and small across the rocky ridgelines and wooded mountainsides, perfecting his tracking skills and keen ability to spot what many of us never see. It was once said that the artist could identify approaching hummingbirds from two counties away with one eye, while tracking a fast-moving, bouncing black bear on a pogo stick with the other eye.

Despite his many accomplishments, his most important discovery and skill is the ability to spot the deceptive BigFoot that walks among us but remains unseen by most. After spending decades learning the habits of this elusive, mythical creature, the tracker/artist has finally agreed to share his journals that capture the sightings of the infamous, larger-than-life creature that has mystified generations.

Now you have the opportunity to sharpen your search-and-find skills by finding not only BigFoot and his legendary footprint but also the many other unusual and sometimes unexpected people, creatures, and objects that can be found at anytime . . . anywhere.

Happy Searching!